A Yorkshire range in the kitchen of a farmhouse near Todmorden, West Yorkshire.

FIREGRATES AND KITCHEN RANGES

David J. Eveleigh

Shire Publications Ltd

CONTENTS

Printed in Great Britain by C. I. Thomas & Sons (Haverfordwest) Ltd, Press Buildings, Merlins Bridge, Haverfordwest, Dyfed SA61 1XF.

ACKNOWLEDGEMENTS
Illustrations are acknowledged as follows: Aga-Rayburn, Glynwed Appliances Ltd, page 30; Bath Museums Service, pages 3, 5 (both), 6 (right); Bath Reference Library, page 2; Beamish, The North of England Open Air Museum, pages 15, 21; Bodleian Library, page 16; Jonathan Brown, page 10; Buckinghamshire County Museum, page 13 (lower left); Castle Museum, York, pages 14 (top), 20 (bottom); Ray Miller, front cover; Museum of English Rural Life, pages 7 (top right), 11, 24, 25 (bottom), 26, 27, 29; Oxfordshire Museum Service, page 23; Keith Robinson, pages 6 (left), 12 (lower two), 13 (top and bottom left); Crown copyright, Science Museum, London, page 18 (bottom).

COVER: *The Hattersley range at the Cogges Farm Museum, Witney, Oxfordshire. See page 23 for details.*

BELOW: *A freestanding grate from 'The Stove Grate Maker's Assistant' (1771) by William Glossop.*

London, Published as the Act directs Feb 1. 1771, by I.Taylor.

A Bath pattern hob grate, late eighteenth century.

INTRODUCTION

Firegrates are not an essential part of a fireplace unless coal is burned. Wood will burn on an open hearth, supported by a pair of firedogs, but coal needs to be contained in a compact mass so that enough heat will be generated for its combustion. So the grate evolved as a container raised above the hearth with a bottom grating so that the ashes could fall away and prevent the fire from choking.

The early history of grates is obscure since early examples which can be dated with certainty are not known. But from the sixteenth century references to grates occur in inventories. Probate inventories exist in large numbers for the period roughly between 1550 and 1750. They list household contents and constitute an important source for the early history of the grate. They show that in areas where coal was found grates were common. The published series of inventories for Telford, which partly coincides with the east Shropshire coalfield, indicates that by 1660 coal was burnt in grates in most homes.

Away from mining districts coal was expensive and wood and turf were more usual fuels. Peter Kahm, a Swedish botanist who visited Essex in 1747, reported that although coal was the common fuel in London it had given way to wood no more than 14 miles (23 km) outside the city. Kahm's observation is borne out by another series of inventories, for Writtle in Essex, which cover the period 1635 to 1747. Grates are recorded only five times in these, and most fireplaces simply had a pair of firedogs for wood.

The grates listed in inventories are rarely described in detail, though the survival of primitive examples, possibly several hundred years old, provides a basis for speculating on their form. Such grates are simply rectangular baskets of wrought iron attached to vertical standards which resemble the uprights of firedogs. The first domestic grates might well have been made by joining firedogs together with horizontal bars.

Inventories are more useful in indicating the use of the grate. Most grates occur as part of the contents of the kitchen, and so it is clear that they were used for cooking. Yorkshire inventories of the seventeenth century describe kitchen grates as *ranges,* and by the eighteenth century this term had become general for grates intended for cooking. Inventories after 1700 occasionally record grates in other parts of the house such as the parlour and upstairs rooms. They were usually known as *stove grates* and this term was universal throughout the eighteenth and nineteenth centuries for drawing-room grates.

STOVE GRATES 1700-1860

By the early eighteenth century some London ironmongers and braziers were using the stove grate as their trade emblem. Coal, brought by sea from Newcastle, had long been used for domestic purposes in London because of the scarcity of wood. Stove grates of this period consisted of freestanding containers with front bars of bright steel. They were supported by ornate standards of cast brass and normally fitted with an iron plate at the back to protect the fireplace from damage by heat. Grates of this form are illustrated in *The Stove Grate Maker's Assistant,* published by William Glossop in 1771.

Glossop's book also includes a few examples of *hob grates,* which became a very common design during the late eighteenth century. Hob grates were set into the fireplace and were not freestanding like the earlier type. The fire bars were flanked by two plates which extended to the sides of the fireplace. The front plates were surmounted by hobs on a level with the top fire bar, and these provided a useful surface for boiling kettles. Hob grates were of three forms, Bath, Pantheon and Forest, distinguishable by the shape of the front plates.

There are rare examples of hob grates cast in brass, but by the 1770s they were manufactured mainly by the iron foundries. In the early eighteenth century most iron, smelted from ore, was converted to wrought iron as the molten metal was of poor quality and had limited application. Abraham Darby, an ironfounder, moved to Coalbrookdale in Shropshire in 1708, and shortly afterwards pioneered the smelting of iron by coke. This produced a hotter molten iron of much better quality since most of the impurities were burnt out. It was now possible to pour the molten iron into enclosed moulds capable of producing finer castings than hitherto.

The Dale Company of Coalbrookdale produced many hob grates, but surviving examples often bear the mark of the Carron Company, which was established near Falkirk in 1759. It employed John Adam and the Haworth brothers, William and Henry, to design many of their products. They were exponents of the neo-classical style, and many Carron hob grates, and indeed many from other works, are embellished with elegant neo-classical motifs. Carron and Dale are the two firms most closely associated with the early manufacture of cast iron grates. But they also supplied pig iron to other smaller foundries, which used cupola furnaces to remelt the iron. By the early nineteenth century there were many smaller foundries in towns throughout Britain manufacturing cast iron stove grates, ovens and kitchen ranges.

Throughout the eighteenth and nineteenth centuries a smoky chimney was a common cause for complaint against domestic fireplaces. The problem was more acute if coal was burnt as the thick black sulphurous smoke could make the atmosphere of a room unbearable if it was not drawn up the chimney. The fault lay not so much with the grate as with the flue above, but attempts to remedy the problem influenced grate design.

The huge dimensions of fireplaces for wood fires were greatly reduced with the introduction of a grate, but the wide

ABOVE: *A Pantheon pattern hob grate, late eighteenth century.*
BELOW: *A Forest pattern hob grate, late eighteenth century.*

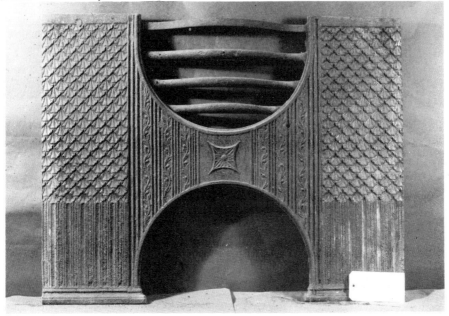

LEFT: *A Forest grate, showing the height of the fire from the hearth.*
RIGHT: *A small Bath grate typical of those found in bedrooms.*

entrance into the chimney was left un-altered. Consequently the draught tended to be sluggish and was often countered by downdraughts which blew the smoke back into the room. A simple device for concentrating the draught was a vertical iron plate which closed the upper part of the fireplace except for an arched opening above the grate. This was drastic enough to cure any smoky chimney, but the cost was huge coal consumption as the fire burned away very quickly. All the heated air disappeared up the chimney, drawing in a cold current in its place. The result was 'a roaring fire that will melt gold, and a room in which no corner will be without its cutting current'.

A finer adjustment of the chimney opening was required if the smoke was to escape without drawing away all the heated air. The answer was to fit a movable iron plate in the chimney above the grate which could adjust the size of the opening into the chimney. These iron doors were called *registers* and, although the principle had long been known, they became common only after 1750. The register gave its name to a type of grate, which, unlike others, occupied the entire fireplace. *Register grates* had back and side plates extending upwards to the chimney opening. On their top rested the register door, which, when closed, entirely sealed off the chimney. They were typically finished in an expensive style with decorative front bars of polished steel.

When the fire was first lit the register door was left fully open to give unrestricted passage to the smoke up the chimney, but once the fire was well established the opening was reduced to keep the loss of heated air, and the cold draughts, to a minimum. Despite the addition of the door, register grates were far from efficient. The grate was placed close to the chimney opening, causing too strong a draught. The fire burned too quickly, but because of the distance of the grate from the hearth the air near the floor remained unheated.

These and other shortcomings were the subject of an essay published in 1797 by Count Rumford, an American statesman,

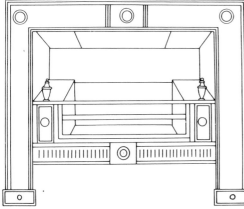 

LEFT: *A typical late eighteenth-century register grate, redrawn from a patent of 1795.*
RIGHT: *A trade token, issued by Skidmore of High Holborn in 1795, showing a register grate.*

soldier and inventor. To solve the problem of smoky chimneys, Rumford rejected the register door in favour of contracting the chimney opening to a depth of 4 inches (100 mm). He also lowered the grate so that the floor might be warmed. This also increased the distance between the fire and the chimney opening so that the draught, although concentrated by the smaller passage, was not too strong. Smoky chimneys were cured, the fire burned more efficiently, and undue currents of cold air were avoided.

Rumford observed that so long as fires remained open to the chimney most of the air heated by the fire would be drawn up the chimney. Rooms were warmed not so much by hot air as by heat radiated from the fire and the sides of the grate. Rumford found that the deep sides of register and other grates and fireplaces were ill designed for reflecting the heat into the room. So he reduced the depth of the fireplace by bringing the back forward and inclined the sides to the back at an angle of about 135 degrees. This reduced the grate area but increased its reflective capacity. Rumford rejected the use of iron for these surfaces as they absorbed too much heat. He recommended constructing the sides of a non-conducting material such as firebrick as this would reflect more efficiently.

Some existing fireplaces were modified according to Rumford's specifications, and his essay more generally influenced grate design. By the first decade of the nineteenth century register grates were being made with inclined sides and grates set lower. The front frame continued to be a near square, and this form remained

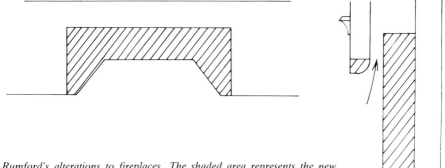

Rumford's alterations to fireplaces. The shaded area represents the new brickwork required to contract the space to the Count's specifications.

LEFT: *Models of grates, no more than 8 inches (200 mm) high are occasionally found. They usually carry coats of arms or rustic figures on top and were clearly intended as ornaments. This example is an accurate representation of a register grate of c 1830, but it has lost its decorative top.*
RIGHT: *A register grate of c 1830. The florid decoration of acanthus leaves on the front plate is typical of this period. The sides are inclined to the back, and the inner back is perforated with holes to allow air to reach the back of the fire.*

popular for grates with or without a register door until the mid nineteenth century. Although grates were frequently advertised as 'Rumfordised', much of the Count's advice went unheeded. For draught control the register door was preferred to the narrowing of the chimney opening, and his recommendation that the fire should burn against firebrick was largely disregarded until later in the century. For a long time it was firmly believed that only grates of iron could be sufficiently decorated to make them acceptable in well furnished rooms.

Nonetheless, improvement of the reflective capacity of grates remained a prime object and in the 1850s was the cause of a major change in shape. At the Great Exhibition in 1851 a novel grate described as the 'heat and light reflecting stove', manufactured by Jobson and Company of Sheffield, attracted considerable attention. The fire was surrounded by a circular plate of polished steel. The high cost of this grate probably prevented its success but shortly afterwards grates framed by arched sides appeared under the name of 'Avon plate reflecting grates'. By 1860 the arched

frame had largely superseded the former square form.

Besides the interest in reflected heat, grates were made which aimed to heat the air of the room. *Hot air grates,* as they were known, had a chamber behind the grate into which fresh air from an external source was admitted. After being warmed in the chamber, the air entered the room through apertures in front. One idea behind their use was to utilise the heat normally lost to the chimney. A Frenchman, Cardinal Polignac, described a fireplace on this principle in his *Le Mechanique à Feu* published in 1713. Three years later this book appeared in English, and Dr Desqualiers, its translator, was responsible for introducing these grates in some London houses. Their use met with considerable prejudice, but in 1742 Benjamin Franklin introduced his *Pennsylvanian* fireplace, which was based on Polignac's invention. In 1753 J. Durno, a London ironmonger, started manufacturing a grate based on Franklin's design, adapted for coal. J. C. Loudon, the architect, writing in 1833, reported seeing Pennsylvanian fireplaces in some Kentish farmhouses. However,

Patterns for grates often remained current over long periods. This register grate, with side hobs, appears in an ironmonger's catalogue of 1896 but the design probably dates from the mid nineteenth century.

The Patent Vesta Register Grate, introduced by the Derwent Foundry Company, Derby, in 1861. This grate is of the arch plate form which became popular in the 1850s. The inner back is lined with firebrick, which is corrugated to allow a passage of air to the back of the fire. This became increasingly common after c 1850.

hot air grates were expensive and their effectiveness was debatable, yet they were made by several firms until the late nineteenth century.

Curing smoky chimneys cleared rooms of smoke, only to pour it into the atmosphere, and in towns and cities this was the cause of asphyxiating fogs. In Leeds, for example, it was estimated in 1910 that the waste of fuel amounted to 20 tons of unburnt coal discharged into the atmosphere every twelve hours. Soot and smoke were proof of the enormous waste and inefficiency of ordinary domestic grates. Efficiency of combustion varied with a coal fire but was at its greatest about an hour after it had been lit. By this time the fire burned bright on top with little or no smoke because a high enough temperature and sufficient quantity of air were present at the surface to ensure complete combustion. But whenever a large mass of fresh fuel was thrown on to the fire the temperature was reduced and the air supply choked. Consequently gases released from the fresh coal as it was heated did not meet with enough air to ignite and passed into the chimney as smoke, cooled below their ignition point.

Numerous attempts were made to design grates in which the fire burned more constantly and efficiently: they were commonly known as *smoke-consuming grates*. One idea was to force the smoke downwards so that it was consumed in the fire before reaching the chimney, but little practical success was achieved with this method. More successful were the grates designed to receive fresh fuel from below, so that the fire always burned efficiently on top. In 1856 William Young invented a grate which was fitted with a large revolving screw which fed coal to the bottom of the fire as it was turned: this device was fitted to some kitchen ranges. Other grates were made with a chamber large enough to hold a day's supply of coal. This was fitted with a movable bottom which could be raised to bring fresh coal to the level of the fire on top. This method was invented by John Cutler in 1815, but it was not until Dr Neil Arnott improved the mechanism in 1854 that this grate achieved a degree of success. But the Arnott and other smoke-consuming grates were complex and expensive, and the building trade, the chief customers of the manufacturers, preferred to buy the cheapest varieties.

An arch plate register grate found in a derelict farmhouse near Reading. The top fire bar is fitted with trivets at either end.

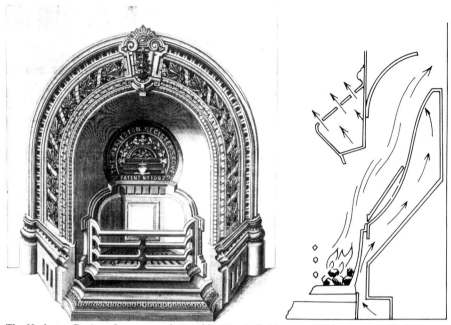

The Harleston Register Stove, manufactured by Marshall, Watson and Moorland of Sheffield, was patented in 1873. Air was supplied to the chamber from an external source and after being heated escaped through apertures in the decorative arched canopy. The canopy also heated air which was drawn in through the vents either side of the fire.

GRATES AFTER 1860

A simpler and equally effective way to achieve more complete combustion and therefore less smoke was to line the grate with firebrick. As Count Rumford had observed, fires were cooled by contact with iron surfaces whereas firebrick grates kept the temperature hotter, producing a more complete combustion.

Iron-framed grates with firebrick linings became increasingly common after 1850 but a more radical development was the *slow combustion grate*, which appeared around 1870. The essential difference was the replacement of the bottom grate with a solid base of firebrick. This cut off the supply of air from below, which in ordinary grates caused the fire to burn quickly and incompletely. The solid base also kept the fire hotter, with the result that combustion was more complete and the cinders were reduced to a fine ash. Nevertheless the successful performance of grates with solid bottoms depended on good quality coal, or else an accumulation of ashes choked the fire. An improved arrangement which had become general by 1900 was to retain the bottom grating but prevent the updraught by filling the space under the fire with a close-fitting ash pan. They were usually supplied with a regulator to admit more air if required.

The slow combustion grates introduced a new shape to fireplaces. The arched frame was replaced by a much smaller rectangular opening. The amount of decorative cast iron was in many instances reduced by the use of glazed tiles for the surround. Hearths, too, were increasingly tiled and this caused a decline in iron

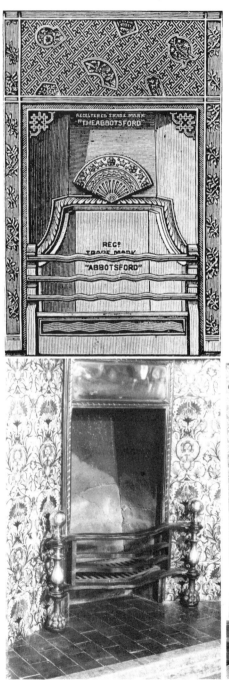

LEFT: *The Abbotsford slow combustion grate, introduced c 1870, was one of the earliest to have the fire lowered almost to the level of the hearth and provided with a solid bottom to cut off air from below.*

BOTTOM LEFT: *From the 1870s there was a revival of eighteenth-century basket grates under the name of dog grates. This one is in a house built in Reading in 1880. The brass standards and steel bars recall eighteenth-century design, but the small rectangular opening and the firebrick lining conform with the latest ideas. The tiles are by William De Morgan.*

BELOW: *A late nineteenth-century register grate with fixed canopy and ash pan.*

and brass fenders. Another change in appearance was caused by the addition around 1880 of a hood or canopy. The growing tendency to bring the grate forward of the chimney opening made a canopy an essential addition to collect the smoke. Many canopies were adjustable to allow a finer control of the draught. Around 1900 adjustable canopies of brass or 'antique' copper pressed with delicate *art nouveau* patterns appeared.

RIGHT: *A grate in a house built in Reading c 1898. The canopy is adjustable but the ash pan is a later type.*

BOTTOM RIGHT: *The Peveril grate, made by R. Russell and Sons, Derby, and introduced in 1904, was one of a number of barless grates popular in the early twentieth century. Front bars obstructed the passage of radiant heat, so they were removed to expose more of the fire to the room. The fire is also well forward of the chimney opening and so is fitted with an adjustable canopy of brass.*

BELOW: *A kitchen grate formerly in the Old Beams Restaurant, Market Square, Aylesbury, Buckinghamshire. The grate stands 810 mm (32 inches) high and is 1090 mm (43 inches) wide. The side cheeks are adjustable. This grate is very similar to the one in the Castle Museum, York, originally from Seaton Delaval Hall, Northumberland.*

ABOVE: *A late eighteenth-century kitchen grate with cast iron hobs.*

BELOW: *An open range provides comfort for the cook and maid in a moment of relaxation. The meat is roasting in front of the fire suspended from a bottle jack. From 'Punch', 1853.*

The fireplace in the Wagon and Horses inn, Saltersgate, North Yorkshire. The turf fire is burning on an iron hearth plate. The oven, which has its own grate, was made by T. Dobson, ironfounder in nearby Pickering.

OPEN RANGES

The development of the kitchen range can be traced without difficulty to the late seventeenth century. The usual form at this period consisted of a cradle-like grate made of horizontal wrought iron bars fixed to four stout legs. The grate was not freestanding but secured by tie bars to the back of the fireplace. The grate was shallow from front to back, but high and broad across the front, making it ideal for roasting. The width of the fire could be adjusted by movable sides, known as cheeks, which were wound in and out by a rack and pinion. On some examples the top front bar folded down when a deep fire was not required. This fall bar provided a convenient place for pots and kettles to simmer in front of the fire. *Trivets,* circular iron rings big enough to support a kettle, were attached to the top of the cheeks and made to swing out over the fire. An early example which can be dated belongs to the Castle Museum, York: it was made for Seaton Delaval Hall in Northumberland between 1718

and 1729.

The next development, which occurred sometime after 1750, was a consequence of the increasing number of iron foundries capable of producing good quality but cheap castings. The spaces either side of the grate were replaced with cast iron panels with hobs on top. The winding cheeks retracted under the hobs, giving the range a much neater appearance. Eighteenth-century ranges were commonly placed in a low chimney opening, which caused a strong draught. This was put to good use by means of *smoke jacks,* which were used to turn the spit: tin-plated vanes placed in the chimney above the fire were rotated by the draught and a series of gears, pulleys and chains transmitted the motion to the spit.

The early iron foundries soon began to produce iron baking ovens. The traditional *beehive oven,* so called from the shape of its cavity in the wall, suffered from the limitation that it had to be reheated between batches. The new cast

15

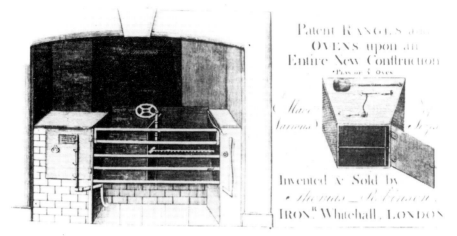

Thomas Robinson's range as described in his patent of 1780, from an advertisement sheet.

iron ovens were often described as 'perpetual' because heat could be maintained by the grate which was included underneath. A flue ran from the grate around the sides and back of the oven, providing a more constant and even heat than could be attained with the traditional ovens.

These iron ovens were often built into a fireplace to one side of the main kitchen grate. The logical development was to unite oven and kitchen grate, so that the former no longer required a separate fire. Ironfounders started making ranges on this plan around 1770, although who did so first is not known. The earliest description of one occurs in a patent taken out by Thomas Robinson, a London ironmonger, in 1780. The oven was fitted in the space formerly occupied by one of the side hobs. Soon after, the space of the other hob was replaced by a boiler. The patent of Joseph Langmead, a London ironfounder, taken out in 1783, was the first to specify this type of range.

This completed the basic development of the open kitchen range, familiar in so many kitchens for the next hundred years. As the fire remained open to the chimney, a crane was still required to suspend pots and kettles. The swinging trivet and fall bar were also retained. The range continued to be used for open fire roasting although the restricted width of

grates in smaller ranges made it necessary to roast on a vertical axis. Around 1790 clockwork *bottle jacks* were introduced to suspend the meat and turn it in front of the fire. However, wide roasting ranges complete with smoke jack continued to be used in large establishments into the twentieth century.

The oven described in Robinson's patent of 1780 was heated through one side always being in contact with the grate. The ovens of some ranges had a projection of solid cast iron attached to the side nearest the fire to improve the conduction of heat. They were sometimes known as *poker ovens*, but they tended to heat unequally, the side nearest the fire being scorched while the other remained cool. A better arrangement was to provide a flue around the oven. These *hot air ovens* were controlled by *dampers*, sliding or pivoted metal plates, operated by hand, which could be opened to draw the hot air through the flue or closed to shut it off.

The addition of a rectangular boiler to the kitchen range was a great improvement in the provision of hot water. Previously it had been necessary to place a large portable boiler of iron or copper over the fire. The simplest boilers attached to ranges were filled and emptied through a lid on top, but others

An open range with oven and boiler made by the Coalbrookdale Company, in a farmhouse near Bridgnorth, Shropshire. According to a circular badge on the boiler, this design was registered in 1869.

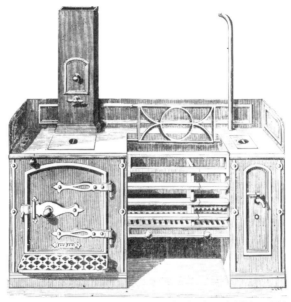

ABOVE: *An open range with oven, L boiler, adjustable cheek and fall bar. This range appears in the 1881 catalogue of Barnard, Bishop and Barnards, Norwich, but apart from a few details is identical to those of the early nineteenth century.*

BELOW: *This large roasting range was installed by Benham and Sons in the Skinners' Company Hall in Dowgate Hill, London EC, as recently as 1907. The gears of the smoke jack, which turn the spits, can be seen at the top. This range is now an exhibit at the Science Museum, London.*

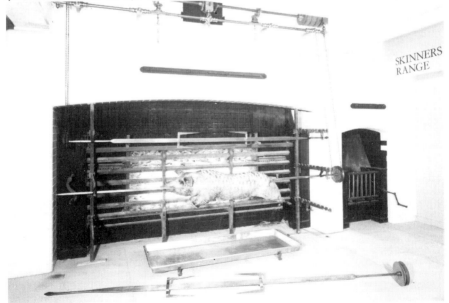

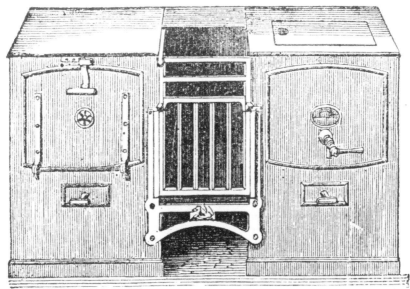

The Newark cottage range made by Nicholson of Newark-on-Trent, Nottinghamshire, was introduced in the 1840s. The Society for Improving the Condition of the Labouring Classes recommended its adoption in 1848 and many were installed in model homes built for the poor in London.

were provided with a tap. Many ranges retained a movable cheek on the boiler side of the grate; this, if wound in to reduce the fire, would prevent heat reaching the water. This problem was solved by making the boiler L-shaped so that it extended to the back of the grate, ensuring that part of it was always within reach of the fire. In ranges with very wide grates primarily intended for roasting large joints the boiler was placed entirely at the back since insufficient room was left at the side. These could not be filled by hand and so they were controlled by a cistern and ballcock.

These essential technical developments had occurred by about 1815 but to what extent were they adopted? At first their use was probably confined to districts in or near to coalfields, where simpler kitchen grates, without ovens and boilers, were already common. A rare comment on this is provided by John Farey, writing on Derbyshire in 1813: 'About the year 1778, cast iron ovens began to be made at the Griffin Foundry, now Messrs Ebenezer Smith and Company, and to be set by the sides of the grates at the public houses

and some farm houses, so as to be heated by the fire in the grate when a small damper in the flue is drawn, and about ten years after, square iron boilers with lids were introduced to be set at the end of a fire grate and these have spread so amazingly that there is scarcely a house without these.' John Smith, father of Ebenezer, began business at the Griffin Foundry in 1775. The works were typical of many other foundries established in the north of England and manufacturing ranges from the late eighteenth century. London, too, was a centre of range manufacture by 1800.

In other parts of Britain, especially the southern counties, wood continued to be used for domestic fires, and many farmhouses and cottages retained the large old chimney fireplaces, cooking being done over the open hearth. Coal gradually became more widely available in the nineteenth century as improvements in transport brought about a reduction in its price, but the introduction of ranges was governed by other factors. In working class homes especially, the progress of ranges was slow because they were re-

LEFT: *A small open range in a cottage near Bridgnorth, Shropshire. This range has only an oven. The blank panel on the other side of the grate was generally known as a 'sham'.*

BELOW: *The Albert Kitchener, a Yorkshire type range made by William Thomlinson Walker at the Victoria Ironworks, York. Yorkshire ranges similar to this were being made by at latest the 1820s but Walker did not introduce his Albert Kitchener until the mid 1860s. Formerly in a house in York, it is now on display in the city's Castle Museum.*

garded as a landlord's fixture. Poor families, in town and country alike, often had to make do with an iron pot suspended over a simple grate. Nevertheless, after about 1850, new working class homes were usually fitted with ranges that had at least a small oven.

Ranges of a similar design were found all over Britain. The sales of the large makers were wide. For example, ranges made by the Coalbrookdale Company have been discovered in homes as far apart as Sussex and Dyfed in Wales. Equally, the large firms based in London, the Midlands, South Yorkshire and Scotland distributed their ranges throughout Britain. However, there were types confined to certain areas, and this can be accounted for by numerous small foundries whose ranges were sold only locally.

Ranges in Yorkshire and other parts of the north of England followed a different development. Whereas most had the boiler and oven at the same level as the grate, the *Yorkshire range* was characterised by an oven set above the level of the fire. This was a natural development of an earlier arrangement where separate iron ovens had been placed high up to one side of the main grate.

The interior of a cottage at Shiremoor, Tyne and Wear, in 1964. The range has a circular oven door, which is a characteristic feature of ranges in north-east England.

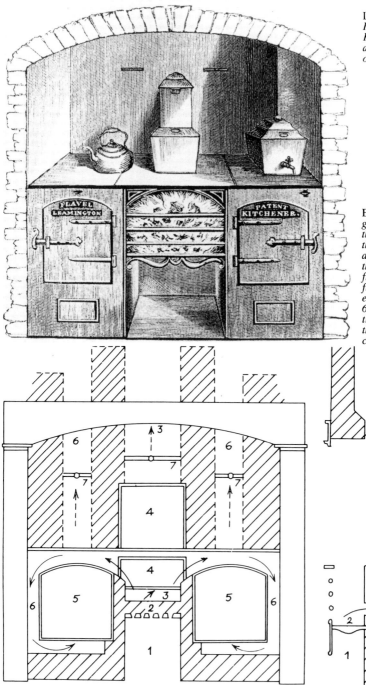

LEFT: *William Flavel's Patent Kitchener, from an advertisement of 1829.*

BELOW: *Diagrams showing the direction of the flues around a closed range: 1, the ash pit; 2, the fire; 3, the boiler flue; 4, the boiler; 5, the ovens; 6, oven flues; 7, the damper; 8, the register in the chimney.*

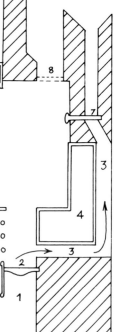

The Hattersley range, patented in 1890, is a typical closed type with two ovens for roasting and baking. The flues for the two ovens were frequently arranged so that the one around the baking oven passed underneath first, providing bottom heat, which was more suitable for baking, whilst the flue of the roasting oven passed over the top first, providing top heat. The cook is seen drawing the damper for the roasting oven flue. This range can be seen at Cogges Farm Museum, Witney, Oxfordshire, and is occasionally used for cooking demonstrations.

CLOSED RANGES

Open ranges continued to be made throughout the nineteenth century, but their inefficiency was often a cause for complaint. In 1796 Count Rumford criticised the enormous quantity of fuel which was consumed in the large open grates. Too much heat went straight up the chimney without serving any purpose. 'More fuel', Rumford observed, 'is frequently consumed in a kitchen range to boil a tea kettle than with proper management would be sufficient to cook a dinner for fifty men.' Instead, Rumford advocated an enclosed stove in which every cooking vessel would have its own separate fireplace, so that no more fuel than was absolutely necessary would be burnt, but this was a complicated design and never adopted. Nonetheless some of his principles were incorporated in the *closed range*, which was the principal development of the nineteenth century.

The first patent for a closed range was taken out by George Bodley, an Exeter ironfounder, in 1802. Bodley reduced the size of the grate and covered it with a cast

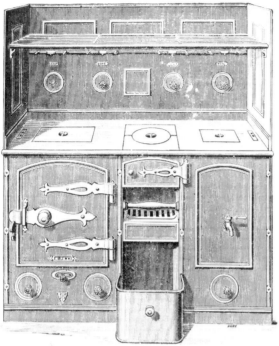

iron plate which prevented the heat ascending the chimney until it had passed through flues surrounding an oven and boiler. As the iron cover was also heated it acted as a hot plate for cooking. In her *Book of Household Management*, Mrs Beeton claimed that the closed range was first used in Devon for the convenience of the hot plate for scalding milk to make clotted cream. However, closed ranges are more usually associated with the Midlands, which became one of the chief areas of their manufacture. William Flavel, who established a foundry in Leamington Spa in the early nineteenth century, began making closed ranges under the name of 'patent kitcheners' in the 1820s. The name endured and closed ranges were generally known as *Leamington kitcheners*. In 1833 J. C. Loudon reported that open ranges were 'entirely laid aside' in favour of kitcheners in villas around Leamington.

Flavel no doubt named his range the kitchener because of its versatility. The large fires of open ranges were suited only to roasting. In some houses the range had to be supplemented by a brick stove burning charcoal, which provided a gentler heat suitable for stewing. However, stews could simmer gently over the fire of a kitchener, protected from too intense a heat by the hot plate. For fast boiling, circular holes with removable lids were provided which exposed the vessels to a higher temperature. Chimney cranes and trivets, therefore, were no longer needed. The closed range was also a much cleaner cooking apparatus. As the smoke passed through flues under the hot plate, the chimney opening above the range was closed off by a register door. Food was no longer in contact with the grime of the fire. Pots and pans were no longer blackened by soot and, being protected from the strongest heat, they lasted longer. The clean space above the hot plate was lined with cast iron covings or glazed tiles and used for the warming of plates.

A greater economy of fuel in closed ranges was attributed to the much reduced grate. They were therefore less suited to roasting in front of the fire than

RIGHT: *Taken from an iron-monger's cata-logue of 1896, these two illustra-tions show how a closed range was converted to an open type.*

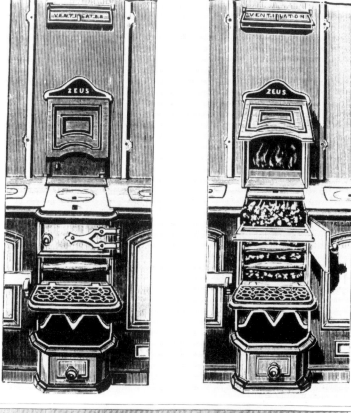

BELOW: *Very large ranges, such as this one from the Bar-nard, Bishop and Barnards cata-logue, were in-tended for hotels and restaurants.*

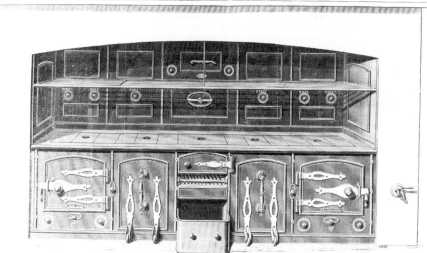

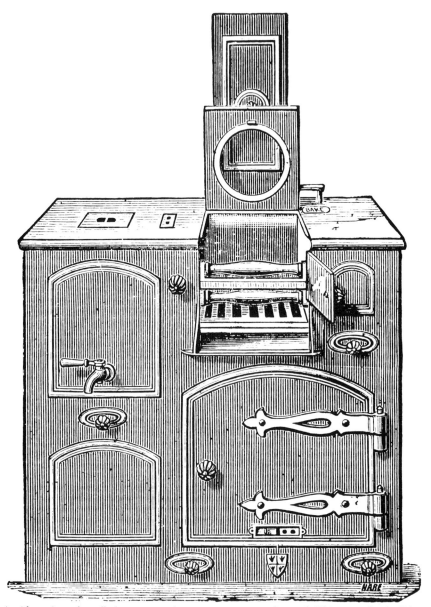

A wide variety of small cheap ranges for cottages was manufactured. This example, the Diamond Cooking Range from the Barnard, Bishop and Barnards catalogue of 1881, was made only 2 feet (610 mm) wide and to save space the grate was placed over the oven.

The Livingstone range was a portable or American stove, manufactured by Murdoch and Company. In an attempt to widen its appeal, the Livingstone range had a fire open at the front which could be used for open roasting, so this illustration from an advertisement of 1874 shows a Dutch oven, complete with bottle jack and roasted meat, standing to the left of the range.

open ranges, so many kitcheners were furnished with a second oven for roasting. Oven-roasted meat was held to be greatly inferior to meat roasted before the fire because the absence of a circulation of hot air prevented the surface of the meat from drying up and browning. Instead the meat was left sodden and it absorbed unpleasant flavours which resulted from melting fat burning in the oven. Count Rumford had shown that meat could be roasted in an oven providing there was a current of hot air. So roasting ovens were provided with a ventilator at the front and an outlet at the back to provide the requisite circulation. Manufacturers also adapted closed

ranges for open fire roasting by making the grate bottom adjustable so that it could be lowered to increase the size of the fire. These grates were operated by a ratchet which enabled the fire to be reduced if less heat was required.

The typical kitchener consisted of two ovens, one each side of the grate, and a boiler behind, each heated by a separate flue. To promote a strong draught, a door in front covering the top of the fire was added. This was closed when heat was required in the flues, but otherwise left open to prevent the fire burning away too quickly. The flues were controlled by dampers, which enabled the heat of the fire to be directed to any part of the range. For example, to heat up the water in the boiler quickly, the door in front was closed, the boiler damper was drawn out, and the other flues were shut off to draw all the heat through the boiler flue. This, however, prevented the ovens being used until the boiler damper was shut. As domestic plumbing increased in the nineteenth century the range was increasingly required to supply hot water for all the house. These conflicting demands remained as long as ranges were used, although boilers placed over the fire and which required no separate flue were applied to some of the later ranges.

Upon close scrutiny the kitchener was revealed to be far from economical. To some extent this was the fault of careless servants who failed to use the dampers correctly. The flues promoted a strong draught and, if left unchecked, this caused an unnecessarily high consumption of coal. But even with correct management, the fire was apt to burn too strongly. Opening the door in front and pushing back the hot plate over the fire when cooking was over did not reduce the draught enough. Coal consumption was very high, and the intense heat wore out the parts in contact with the fire and much expense was incurred in repairs. An effective remedy was to make the closed range convertible to an open type. The *Lichfield range* manufactured by William Carter and Company of Birmingham, patented in 1866, pioneered this development. The central portion of the hot plate was slid back and doors were opened in the back so that the smoke passed directly into the chimney: the flues were thus bypassed and the draught was reduced. By the 1880s most closed ranges were made on this principle.

Another problem experienced with kitcheners was ventilation of the kitchen. In open ranges the steam and smells from cooking were drawn up the chimney with the smoke but in closed ranges the chimney opening was sealed by a register door. If this was opened to expel the air it was likely to interfere with the performance of the flues. Ventilators were added which did not require opening the register but it was essential their exit was above the flues if the draught was not to be checked.

PORTABLE RANGES

All the ranges so far described required setting into the fireplace with brickwork. In 1815 Thomas Deakin, a London ironmonger, patented a portable range, but the type did not become common until an American example was shown at the Great Exhibition in 1851. Consequently they were often known as *American stoves,* although their manufacture was chiefly in Scotland. Some manufacturers, such as Smith and Wellstood, established in 1854 near Falkirk, dealt almost exclusively in portable ranges.

The iron casing of portable stoves entirely enclosed the fire and flues, and this promoted a more efficient use of heat. They stood on four legs and could be placed in the middle of the room, providing an iron flue pipe connected the stove with the chimney or outside wall. Although small and compact, portable stoves usually had an oven, boiler and a hot plate on top. However, the English predilection for open fires restricted their popularity.

By the beginning of the twentieth century gas and later electricity were becoming serious rivals to coal ranges, yet developments continued. Portable ranges burning anthracite were introduced. One popular type was the Kooksjoie made by the London Warming Company. Although more expensive than ordinary fuel, anthracite produced very little soot and ash and burned very slowly. In 1929 the Aga cooker, invented by a Swede, Dr Gustave Dalen, was introduced to England. The Aga was designed to burn coke but through automatic draught control and careful insulation it was extremely economical. But the Aga was expensive, and by the 1930s gas and electric cookers were firmly established as the modern alternatives to the kitchen range.

A small portable range, standing in a former open fireplace.

Modern cleanliness and efficiency in the form of an Aga cooker.

FURTHER READING

Beeton, Isabella. *Mrs Beeton's Book of Household Management*. Ward Lock and Bowden, 1907.

Bernan, W. *The History and Art of Warming and Ventilating Rooms and Buildings*. Bell, 1845.

Brears, P. *The Kitchen Catalogue*. York Castle Museum, 1979.

Brears, P. *Traditional Food in Yorkshire*. John Donald, 1987.

Edwards, F. *Our Domestic Fireplaces*. Hardwick, second edition 1865.

Edwards, F. *On the Extravagant Use of Fuel in Cooking*. Hardwick, 1869.

Glossop, W. *The Stove Grate Maker's Assistant*. Taylor, 1771.

Loudon, J. C. *Cottage, Farm and Villa Architecture*. Longman, 1833.

Phillips, R. Randal. *The Servantless House*. Country Life, 1920.

Rumford, Count. *Essay X on the Construction of Kitchen Fireplaces*. T. Cadell and W. Davies, 1799.

Teale, T. P. *Economy of Coal in House Fires*. Churchill, 1883.

Webster, T. *An Encyclopaedia of Domestic Economy*. Longman, 1844.

Cleaning the iron drawing-room grates and the kitchen range was a tedious business. In wealthier homes this was one of the maid's duties and she might have been equipped with a housemaid's box such as this. The bottom was used for collecting cinders from the fire and the tray on top held stove brushes and blacklead to polish the iron surfaces. The bright parts, handles and hinges were burnished with emery cloth or brick dust and paraffin. In addition the flues of the range had to be regularly cleared of soot.

PLACES TO VISIT

Intending visitors are advised to check times of opening before making a special journey.

Abbeydale Industrial Hamlet, Abbeydale Road South, Sheffield S7 2QW. Telephone: 0742 367731.

Abbey House Museum, Kirkstall, Leeds LS5 3GH. Telephone: 0532 755821.

Beamish: The North of England Open Air Museum, Beamish, Stanley, County Durham DH9 0RG. Telephone: 0207 231811.

Blackburn Museum and Art Gallery, Museum Street, Blackburn, Lancashire BB1 7AJ. Telephone: 0254 667130.

Blaise Castle House Museum, Henbury, Bristol BS10 7QS. Telephone: 0272 506789.

Bridewell Museum of Norwich Trades and Industries, Bridewell Alley, Norwich, Norfolk NR2 1AQ. Telephone: 0603 667228.

Cambridge and County Folk Museum, 2/3 Castle Street, Cambridge CB3 0AQ. Telephone: 0223 355159.

Clitheroe Castle Museum, Castle Hill, Clitheroe, Lancashire BB7 1BA. Telephone: 0200 24635.

Coalbrookdale Museum of Iron and Furnace, Coalbrookdale, Ironbridge, Telford, Shropshire. Telephone: 0952 433418.

Cogges Farm Museum, Church Lane, Cogges, Witney, Oxfordshire OX8 6LA. Telephone: 0993 772602.

Elvaston Working Estate Museum, Elvaston Castle, Elvaston, Derby DE7 3EP. Telephone: 0332 573799.

Erddig, Wrexham, Clwyd LL13 0YT. Telephone: 0978 355314.

Georgian House, 7 Great George Street, Bristol BS1 5RR. Telephone: 0272 211362.

Grosvenor Museum, 27 Grosvenor Street, Chester, Cheshire CH1 2DD. Telephone: 0244 321616.

Morwellham Quay Open Air Museum, Morwellham, Tavistock, Devon PL19 8JL. Telephone: 0822 832766.

Number 1, Royal Crescent, Bath, Avon. Telephone: 0225 428126.

Old House Museum, Cunningham Place, Bakewell, Derbyshire.

Ordsall Hall Museum, Taylorson Street, Salford, Lancashire M5 3EX. Telephone: 061-872 0251.

Pendle Heritage Centre, Park Hill, Barrowford, Nelson, Lancashire BB9 6JQ. Telephone: 0282 695366.

People's Palace Museum, Glasgow Green, Glasgow G40 1AT. Telephone: 041-554 0223.

Pontefract Museum, Salter Row, Pontefract, West Yorkshire WF8 1BA. Telephone: 0977 797289.

Somerset Rural Life Museum, Abbey Farm, Chilkwell Street, Glastonbury, Somerset BA6 8DB. Telephone: 0458 31197.

Staffordshire County Museum, Shugborough, Stafford ST17 0XB. Telephone: 0889 881388.

Towneley Hall Art Gallery and Museums, Burnley, Lancashire BB11 3RQ. Telephone: 0282 24213.

Towner Art Gallery and Local History Museum, Manor Gardens/High Street, Old Town, Eastbourne, East Sussex BN20 8BB. Telephone: 0323 411688.

Tudor House Museum, Bugle Street, Southampton, Hampshire. Telephone: 0703 224216.

Watford Museum, 194 High Street, Watford, Hertfordshire WD1 2HG. Telephone: 0923 32297.

Wayside Museum, Zennor, St Ives, Cornwall TR26 3DA. Telephone: 0736 796945.

York Castle Museum, Tower Street, York, North Yorkshire YO1 1RY. Telephone: 0904 653611.